THE AMERICAN PHILOSOPHER SERIES

ORIENTAL PHILOSOPHIES

With an Introduction by

DR. W. Y. EVANS-WENTZ

RUSSELL F. MOORE COMPANY, *Publishers*

80 Wall Street, New York

181

CONTENTS

INTRODUCTION

THE LIGHT FROM THE EAST

"Nothing that is eternal can be gained by what is not eternal."
Mundaka Upanishad

Today, as it did in the days of Pythagoras, of Plato, of Plotinus, of Appolonius of Tyana, and of other truth-seekers who have been the shapers of the culture and faiths of the Occident, "From the Orient cometh the Light."

Increasingly, as the old barrier-walls, built of misunderstandings and prejudices, are overthrown, which too long have been allowed to separate culturally the continent of Europe and the Americas from Asia, will with mutual respect and understanding bind East and West together. Then, in transcendent love, such as overleaps every impediment of creed and caste and race, humanity for the first time in known history will come to realize that it is in reality One Family, that as St. Paul enunciated, we are truly members of One Body. It is only when the West understands the East and the East the West that a social order worthy to be called civilized will be evolved; and by no other means can there come forth a New Age.

Mechanization and atomic power may ameliorate man's life on Earth, but they cannot create culture or emancipate man. Nor can the Occident alone direct the future of human evolution.

Ever since the time of Europe's pioneer thinkers and trained seers, especially Pythagoras and Plotinus and Appolonius of Tyana, each of whom travelled to India to attain guidance in Right Knowledge, the West unceasingly has found its social salvation in oriental culture. When the folk of Western Europe and of the British Isles were barbarians and painted their bodies and wore crude skins of wild beasts, India and China were more culturally advanced than any part of Europe, not excepting Greece and Rome, ever had been prior to our own epoch. Then, with the coming of the Renaissance, which was inspired by the classical culture born of the East, Europe for the first time awakened from its primitiveness and began to understand the significance of culture.

ix

The corpus of teachings which came to be called Christian was itself, as St. Augustine frankly acknowledged, orientally derived; nor were these teachings, as he well knew, something unique or new. Originating from many sources, they transmitted, in large measure, the quintessence of salvation doctrines which, long before the rise of Christianity in the West, were common both to India and to China and in lesser degree to the Mystery Schools of the ancient Egyptian and Grecian and Mediterranean civilizations. Thus, likewise for Christendom, it was through oriental assistance that the Occident was delivered from barbarism.

Almost imperceptibly during a century and more now, or since European scholars began to recognize the importance of the Sacred Books of the East, to which the seven small treatises here before us bear such eloquent witness, the thought of Europe and of the Americas has been profoundly modified by that of the Orient. *The Bhagavad Gita*, the *Upanishads*, the *Diamond Sutra*, the discourses of Confucius and Mencius and Laotze, and the *Dharma* of the Buddha, together with many more of the supreme teachings flowing in from Asia, have become more or less familiar to the peoples of the West. The Oxford *New English Dictionary* incorporates in its pages, as being already anglicized, Sanskrit derived words which a generation ago were popularly quite unknown, such, for example, as karma, guru, Nirvana, and others. We are, indeed, living in the time of a Renaissance far mightier in its cultural influence than that of fifteenth and sixteenth century Europe; for, at that epoch, the Light from the East could but faintly shine through the accumulated gloom inherited from Europe's Dark Ages. Today the sky is less obscured; when, at last, the New Age of at-one-ment of East and West shall dawn, the mists and clouds and darkness will have been dissipated, and the Sun of Right understanding will rise and illuminate a united world.

It is of more than ordinary significance to have received only a few days ago, from a young American returned from the War and now stationed in one of the United States Naval Personnel Separation Centers, these thoughful observations:—

"The importance of scholars' work touching things Asiatic grows with each day. I note an increasing interest in Asia, perhaps in China in particular, due to the fact that many returning service men have had, during their term of service in the Pacific campaigns, more or less contact with Orientals. That is good, for only by such a growth of brotherly feeling for the peoples of the East can future misunderstanding and possible disaster be avoided."

As this aptly suggests, a scholarly presentation in easily comprehended and compact form of the very quintessence of what is best in the cultural heredity of Asia, is of inestimable importance, not only culturally and politically, but in world-wide commercial relationships as well. The very issuance of such publications as *Oriental Philosophies* is an omen of far reaching signification, for it heralds the coming of an age which truly shall be new and great and divinely-guided. There can be no greater social service than that of helping to prepare the way for a civilization which shall be really humanitarian, not merely Eastern or Western, but international.

The whole world faces the most stupendous crisis in all the millenniums. Shall our social order disintegrate as did that of Babylon and Memphis and Rome? Shall all the sacrifices, all the struggles, all the hopes of our forefathers, who with such painful effort built up our Western civilization and made us its heirs, be frustrated? Shall Ignorance continue to shape the policy of so many of our statesmen and religious leaders? Shall we attain a united world and a federation of religions or shall we suffer social disintegration and defeat?

The East has ever extended fraternal greetings to the West. India's and China's culture has gone on unbrokenly for many thousands of years. India has witnessed the fall of the ancient empires of the Occident and of the Near East. Shall its fraternal greetings not be reciprocated by us of this generation? Shall we be faithless custodians of the trust which our ancestors reposed in us? Shall the West, glamourously and hypnotically fettered to its wondrous machines and its utilitarianism, not welcome emancipation; shall it not strive for a new model man more than for a new model car?

The fate of the West will be of its own making. If the Light from the East be allowed to shine unimpededly, its saving power will emancipate the West, for this Light is none other than that of which the Gnostic Christos spoke; it is "the Light which lighteth every man that cometh into the world", be he Christian, Hindu, Buddhist, Jew, Moslem, Taoist, or of any other faith. If, alas, the West rejects the Light, or prevents it from shining clearly, then, once more, chaos will claim Western society. Shall the East once again witness the decline and fall of the West, or shall Western man become sufficiently awakened to avert the cyclic crisis now impending?

If the West is to attain right and lasting greatness, it will not be because of its technology. It must come to realize, as India's Rishis did ages ago, that "Nothing that is eternal can be gained by what is not eternal", that fondness for the transitory and non-eternal leads only to bitter disillusionment. The worldly path was the path which the ancient Romans trod.

Not acquisition of the things which pass away, but their renunciation gives man true power and social stability. Had the Christ chosen worldly dominion, as the Tempter proposed that He should, or had th· Buddha preferred the throne of His father's kingdom rather than the Seat of Buddhahood beneath the Bo-tree in the solitude of the Indian jungle, neither of these Conquerors would have attained the status of Teacher of Gods and Men.

Whereas in the West eager covetousness for and ambitious accumulating and holding fast to the things of this world are inculcated by national systems of education, and are, in fact, the popular practice, in the East the ideal still is, as it was of yore, renunciation. One of my Hindu Gurus, the Late Sj. Atal Bihari Ghosh, has very succinctly set forth this contrasting difference between East and West as follows:—

"The East, even in the days of her material prosperity, never forgot the supremacy of things spiritual. Kings renounced their kingdoms to end their days in meditation, in jungle or mountain solitudes. 'To die in harness' was then, as it still is, an evil to be avoided. Herein lies the secret of the imperishable vitality of the Orient."

As the epitomized treatises which herein follow emphasize, it is not by the conquest of this world, but by the conquest of the animal self that the Great Ones throughout the ages have been empowered to direct the course of human culture and of spiritual enlightenment. And they alone are the world's Heroes, not the captains and their hosts who have ravaged the nations with fire and sword and bloodshed and filled the world with weeping and wailing and dire ruin.

In reading these excellent epitomes of some of the East's most glorious philosophical gifts to the West, I recognize how faithfully they convey that message from the East to the West which is most essential for the West to receive. Having consecrated many of the best years of this incarnation to research in oriental philosophies and religions, I am glad to have the privilege of here setting forth my own appreciation of this supreme message which this little book presents to its readers and through them to the whole Western World, especially America.

May the message be heeded. May the New Age be allowed to come forth in our day from the womb of time. May the spirituality of the East guide the science of the West; may the science of the West assist the East. And may there be throughout the world, encompassing all nations, all continents, all seas and oceans, one nation, one federation, one humanity.

Dr. W. Y. Evans-Wentz

Indian philosophy has been a powerful determinant of Asiatic thought. Through the long centuries its rich spiritual import has trickled into the west by word of mouth, through the writings of scholars, through the translation of books and even by means of the trader's caravans. These heavily laden transports coming from the mysterious depths of India brought more than jewels and spices to the western world: they brought a philosophy older than that of the ancient Greeks! We recognize in the philosophy of India a sensitive and deep appreciation of the eternal problem of man's relation to the spiritual aspects of being.

Indian philosophy is built on the four Vedas: Rig (hymns), Yajur (sacrificial rituals), Sama (liturgies) and Atharva (supernatural rites). The oldest of these Vedas dates from about 6000 B.C. Each has three parts. There are the mantras or hymns, the Brahmanas or religious precepts and the Upanishads or philosophy.

The Upanishads grew from the Vedic hymns and contain the roots of Indian intellectual and spiritual attainment. They are the logical end of the Vedas and are thus termed the "Vedanta." Schopenhauer once remarked of the value of these writings: "In the whole world there is no study so beneficial and elevating as that of the Upanishads."

The authors of the Upanishads are unknown. They were composed sometime during the period from 1000 to 3000 B. C. and while their authorship was doubtless from many hands and over a great number of years they are united in their fundamental teachings.

Thus they hold that the universe is one of change, of creation and dissolution, and one with beginning. This view is reflected in the doctrine of the Trinity of Brahma. There is Brahma the Creator, Vishnu the Maintainer and Shiva the Destroyer. "Brahman" is itself one and neuter and embodies the God-idea or pure essence of being. At the same time it is also conceived as a trinity and the human desire for a personal God is satisfied by these three personal Gods, Brahma, Vishnu and Shiva. The Upanishads are likewise unified in their object, namely, to indicate to man his part in and relationship to the universe. Similarly they all teach the belief of rebirth and pre-existence. Finally while they are all aimed indirectly at an ethical system, ethics as such is not regarded as essential since self-realization is the fundamental sought and ethics is simply a condition met on the way leading to this realization.

The basic problem of the Upanishads and of Indian philosophy in general can be summed up, at the risk of over-simplification, as the problem of the cause and realities of life and death as they relate to man.

Shankara was the most noted of all commentators on the Upanishads. Brahmin of Malabar, he was born about 788 (A. D.) and became noted for his early wisdom and power of Yoga. He wandered from place to place, through the still mountains and forests and through the crowded river villages, sometimes in the company of his friend and disciple Padmapada and sometimes alone. At Benares he wrote his commentary on the Brahman Sutras (short aphorisms expressing philosophical principles), the Upanishads and the Bhagavad Gîta (translated the "Lord's Song" or "Song Celestial"). He died in Kanchi at the age of 32. A profound thinker, his commentaries and teachings based on the Bhagavad Gîta are some of the finest ever written.

Before proceeding to the Bhagavad Gîta, mention should be made of a development of the Vedanta termed "Yoga." Defined very briefly, it consists of a method of ascending to a higher plane of concentration and intelligence. It was codified by Potanjali in the second century B. C. Important as it may be, the Bhagavad Gîta has been selected as more representative of the basic writings of Indian philosophy. Too, the Gîta has been generally accepted by the various schools of Indian philosophy as a work of spiritual authority.

Of this Bhagavad Gîta which appears in the Mahâbharata, one of the two great sacred epics of India, the Indian scholar Swami Bodhananda has made the following enlightening remarks:

This marvelous Sanskrit poem occurs as an episode in the sixth book, the Bhishma Parva, of the Hindu epic—the Mahâbharata—the great store-house of wisdom. The Hindus believe that India attained the very zenith of her power, glory and civilization during the epoch of which the Mahabharata narrates. This epic is called the Hindu Iliad, composed by the Hindu Home, Vyasa.

The central story of the Mahabharata relates, to the rivalry between two branches of cousins entitled to inherit the same ancestral kingdom, and its associated rights and privileges. This rivalry reached its culmination in that great war, at the commencement of which Krishna is said to have taught the Gita to his kinsman, friend and disciple, Arjuna.

The orthodox Hindus believe that this poem of philosophic wisdom has its origin in a discourse between Arjuna and his charioteer Krishna, at the very beginning of a battle which took place on the holy plain of Kurukshetra, situated between two sacred rivers, the Saraswati and the Jumma, in Northwestern India. They also believe that Krishna and Arjuna were historical beings.

Before the commencement of this war, a sage of wonderful powers met the blind king, Dhritarastra, whose sons made up one of the parties of the war, and wished to know if he would like to have his blind eyes opened so that he might be able to see with his own eyes the events of the coming war. The king declined the offer, as he felt that he could not bear the sight of the slaughter of his own kindred, but requested him to so arrange that those events might be fully and accurately reported to him, from time to time. Accordingly, he bestowed the power of supernatural vision upon Sanjaya, a relative of the king, and directed him to report all the details regarding the progress of the war to the blind king.

This king Dhritarastra, though the eldest son of his father, was disqualified from succeeding him on account of his physical deformity, and the younger brother, Pandu, became king. After reigning a number of years, Pandu retired, leaving the throne to his eldest son, Yudhisthira. The blind king had a number of vicious children who became jealous of Yudhisthira and conspired together to dethrone him. Through a series of shameful and inhuman frauds, they succeeded in realising their desires. Yudhisthira and his four brothers, who were famous for such virtues as love, charity and truthfulness, were exiled from the kingdom for a period of twelve years. Taking the opportunity offered by their long absence, the sons of the blind king made their way to the throne and established themselves there. Upon returning from their exile, the five brothers demanded back the kingdom which lawfully belonged to them. They were not only refused, but were bitterly abused by their cousins. Krishna himself went to the court of the sons of Dhritarastra, and proposed an amicable settlement. He advised them to give five small villages to the five Pandava brothers, keeping the rest for themselves. They were, however, so much elated with their success and acquisition that they told Krishna they would not consent to part with an acre of land except by force of arms. On hearing the intentions of their cousins from Krishna, the sons of Pandu prepared to fight for the restoration of their rightful kingdom. Hence arose the war mentioned in the Gita as "Dharmya Yuddha"—Righteous war.

Some scholars among the Hindus themselves give an allegorical interpretation of this warfare. They say that the battle beween the two contending parties stands for the internal battle in man—between his higher nature, conscience, on the one hand, and his lower nature, the passions, on the other. The mythological wars between Ahurmazda and Aharman, are only allegorical expressions of this inner war. The blind king and his children denote, respectively, ignorance and ignorance-begotton vices. The other party represents virtues such as truthfulness, justice, courage, heroism, kindness, etc. Krishna is the Supreme Self and is shown as always on the side of virtue. The heart of man, which is in its own nature pure and unpolluted, is represented by the sacred plain of the holy war. In the war between virtue and vice, virtue wins the victory—the divine triumphs over the animal.

But so far as our practical purposes are concerned, it does not matter at all whether we interpret the Gita literally or symbolically. It is enough for us to know that the teachings contained therein are full of truth and wisdom, and if applied to the details of daily life, can save us from great fear and danger.

Before the actual war began, fear and weakness, in the guise of love and mercy overpowered Arjuna, and he became unwilling to engage in it. He advanced some very plausible reasons against the slaughter and carnage of war. But Krishna, with his divine insight perceived the real feelings of Arjuna's heart, and reproached him for being unsteady, unmanly and unwise. He endeavored to dispel his distress and delusion by a philosophical argument, and to impress upon his mind that it was a sacred duty of his, as a defender of truth and a leader of men, to fight in the cause of justice and righteousness, and that in killing his enemies he would kill their mortal bodies only, and not the imperishable soul. Those mighty words of wisdom still infuse hope and courage and strength into the dullest and feeblest of hearts. "O mighty-armed Arjuna, why has this unworthy weakness come upon thee in this trying situation? Yield not to unmanliness, my child. It does not become thee. Cast off this base weakness of heart, arise and be firm and strong. Do thy duty well and unselfishly. Ever indestructible is this Embodied One in the bodies of all. Thou shouldst not therefore grieve for any living being." The last words of Arjuna after his delusion was gone, were: "Destroyed is ignorance and I have gained wisdom through thy teachings, O Krishna! I am firm with doubts gone. I will do thy biddings. Command me, Sir."

The Gita is a dialogic discourse between Krishna and Arjuna, about the philosophy of conduct, held on the field of battle, the plain of Kurukshetra.

The keynote of this philosophy of conduct is renunciation. It teaches how to abandon all show, selfishness and sensuality, for devotion to unselfish work in the cause of public good; how to keep hearts for God and hands for help; how to live in the world yet not be of it; how to subjugate the animal and manifest the divine in us.

There are eighteen chapters in the Gita—each of which is called a Yoga—a discourse on a certain method of God—realization. The total number of stanzas is about seven hundred; over six hundred of these are the utterances of Krishna, and the rest, of Arjuna, Sanjaya and Dhritarastra. All the most abstruse theories and doctrines regarding religion and philosophy have been discussed and demonstrated between the lines of these chapters. One commentator has remarked that the Gita is such a vast subject that volumes can be written on each single verse of it.

THE BHAGAVAD GITA[1]

Arjuna:

O Krishna, seeing these my kinsmen, gathered here desirous to fight, my limbs fail me, my mouth is parched;

My body shivers, my hair stands on end, my Gandiva (bow) slips from my hand, my skin is burning.

O Keshava (Krishna, the slayer of Keshi), I am not able to stand upright, my mind is in a whirl and I see adverse omens.

O Krishna, neither do I see any good in slaying my own people in this strife. I desire neither victory, nor kingdom, nor pleasures.

Teachers, uncles, sons and grandsons, grandfathers, fathers-in-law, brothers-in-law, besides other kinsmen, for whose sake empire, enjoyment and pleasures are desired, they themselves stand here in battle, forsaking life and wealth. What avail, then, is kingdom, enjoyment, or even life, O Givinda (Krishna)?

These warriors I do not wish to kill, even though I am killed by them, not even for the dominion over the three worlds, how much less for the sake of this earth, O slayer of Madhu.

O Janârdana (giver of prosperity and salvation, Krishna), what pleasure could there be for us by killing the sons of Dhritarâshtra? Sin alone would take possession of us by slaying these evil-doers.

Therefore we ought not to kill these sons of Dhritarâshtra who are our relations; for how can we, O Mâdhava (Krishna), obtain happiness by destroying our own kinsmen?

Although these (my enemies), their understanding being over-powered by greed, see no evil from extinction of families and no sin in hostility to friends.

But, O Janârdana, why should not we turn away from this sin, seeing clearly the evil in destruction of family?

From the destruction of a family the immemorial religious rites of that family perish. Spirituality being destroyed, that whole family is overpowered by unrighteousness.

O Krishna, from the predominance of unrighteousness, the women of that family become corrupt; and women being corrupted, there arises intermingling of castes.

This intermingling of castes leads the destroyers of the family to hell, as also the family itself; for their ancestors fall, being deprived of the offerings of rice ball and water.

By these misdeeds of the slayers of the family, bringing about confusion of casts, the immemorial religious rites of family and caste are destroyed.

O Janârdana, we have heard that for such men, whose household religious rites have been destroyed, the dwelling in hell is inevitable.

Alas! what a great sin we are resolved to incur, being prepared to slay our kinsmen, actuated by greed of kingdom and pleasure.

Verily, it would be better for me if the sons of Dhritarâshtra, weapons in hand, should slay me in the battle, unresisting and unarmed.

Sanjaya:

Speaking thus in the midst of the battlefield, Arjuna sank down on the seat of his war chariot, casting aside his bow and arrows, his mind overwhelmed with sorrow.

Krishna:

O Arjuna, whence comes upon thee in this critical moment this depression unworthy of an Aryan, disgraceful, and contrary to the attainment of heaven?

O son of Prithâ, yield not to unmanliness; it does not befit thee. Casting off this mean faint-heartedness, arise O terror of thy foes!

Arjuna:

O destroyer of enemies and slayer of Madhu (Krishna), how can I fight with arrows in battle against Bhishma and Drona, who are worthy to be worshipped (by me).

Instead of slaying these great-souled masters, it would be better even to live in this life by begging; but killing them, all our enjoyments of wealth and desires, even in this world, will be stained with blood.

Indeed I know not which of the two is better for us, whether we should conquer them or they should conquer us. For those very sons of Dhritarâshtra stand before us, after slaying whom we should not care to live.

With my nature overpowered by pity and depression and mind confused about duty, I implore Thee (O Krishna) tell me with certainty what is good for me. I am Thy disciple, instruct me, who have taken refuge in Thee.

For I see not what can remove this grief which withers my senses, even if I should obtain unrivalled and flourishing dominion over the earth and rulership over the gods.

Sanjaya:

Gudâkesha (Arjuna), the conqueror of his foes, having thus spoken to the Lord of the senses (Krishna), said: "I shall not fight, O Govinda!" and became silent.

O descendant of King Bharata, Hrishikesha (Krishna), as if smilingly, spoke these words to him (Arjuna), who was thus grief-stricken in the midst of the two armies.

Krishna:

Thou hast been mourning for those who should not be mourned for and yet thou speakest (apparent) words of wisdom; but the truly wise mourn not either for the dead or for the living.

It is not that I have never existed before, nor thou, nor all these kings. Nor is that all of us shall cease to exist hereafter.

As in this body the embodied soul passes through childhood, youth and old age, in the same manner it goes from one body to another; therefore the wise are never deluded regarding it (the soul).

O son of Kunti, the feelings of heat, cold, pleasure, pain, are produced from the contact of the senses with sense-objects; they are with beginning and end, transitory. Therefore, O Bhârata, endure them bravely.

O mighty among men, he is fit to attain immortality who is serene and not afflicated by these sensations, but is the same in pleasure and pain.

There is no existence for the unreal and the real can never be non-existent. The Seers of Truth know the nature and final ends of both.

Know That to be indestructible by which all this is pervaded. No one is ever able to destroy that Immutable.

These bodies are perishable; but the dwellers in these bodies are eternal, indestructible and impenetrable. Therefore fight, O descendant of Bhârata!

He who considers this (Self) as a slayer or he who thinks that this (Self) is slain, neither of these knows the Truth. For It does not slay, nor is It slain.

This (Self) is never born, nor does It die, nor after once having been, does It go into non-being. This (Self) is unborn, eternal, changeless, ancient. It is never destroyed even when the body is destroyed.

A son of Pritha, how can he slay or cause the slaying of another who knows this (Self) to be indestructible, eternal, unborn and immutable?

As man casts off worn-out garments and puts on others which are new, similarly the embodied soul casting off worn-out bodies, enters into others which are new.

Sword cannot pierce It (Self), fire cannot burn It, water cannot It and air cannot dry It.

It cannot be pierced, nor burned, nor wet, nor dried. It is eternal, all-pervading, unchangeable, immovable, everlasting.

This (Self) is said to be unmanifested, unthinkable, unchangeable; therefore knowing this to be so, thou shouldst not grieve.

But even if thou thinkest that this (Self) is subject to constant birth and death, even then, O mighty-armed, thou shouldst not grieve.

For that which is born death is certain, and for the dead birth is certain. Therefore grieve not over that which is unavoidable.

O Bhârata, all creatures are unmanifested in the beginning, manifested in their middle state, unmanifested again in the end. What is there to grieve about?

Some look upon It (Self) with wonder, some speak about It with wonder, some hear about It with wonder, some and yet others, even after hearing about It, know It not.

The dweller in the body of everyone is ever indestructible; therefore, O Bhârata, thou shouldst not grieve over any creature. Looking upon it even from this standpoint of thine own Dharma, thou shouldst not waver, for nothing is higher for a Kshatriya (warrior) than a righteous war.

O son of Prithâ, fortunate indeed are Kshatriyas to whom comes unsought, as an open gate to heaven, such a war.

But if thou shouldst not take part in this righteous war, then forfeiting thine own duty and honor, thou shalt incur sin.

People will ever speak ill of thee; for the esteemed, dishonor is even worse than death.

These great car-warriors will think that thou hast withdrawn from the battle through fear. And thou shalt be thought of lightly by those who once honored thee highly.

Thine enemies will speak unutterable disgraceful things against thee and blame thy valor. What can be more painful than this?

If thou fallest in battle, thou shalt obtain heaven; if thou conquerest, thou shalt enjoy the earth. Therefore, O son of Kunti, arise and be resolved to fight.

Regarding alike pleasure and pain, gain and loss, victory and defeat, fight thou the battle. Thus sin will not stain thee.

Thus I have declared unto thee the wisdom of Self-realization.

---

[1] Swami Paramananda, *Srimad-Bhagavad-Gita* (Boston: The Vedanta Centre, 1913), pp. 6-17.

BUDDHA: DHAMMAPADA

Buddha was born about 600 B. C. in the province of Behar in India of a princely family of the warrior caste. In English his name means "The Enlightened." Sensitive to social injustices and to the ills and woes that befall mankind, the young Buddha sought deliverance from a painful existence in the world of men by forsaking his family and position and seeking quiet and meditation in the solitude of the forests. He was 29 at the time of this, the so-called, great renunciation.

He studied from many teachers and became familiar with the Vedas and Upanishads. At length after a number of years of study and concentration he aspired to true wisdom and enlightenment.

He gathered around him numerous disciples, rich and poor, wise and foolish. Having reached complete self-realization he sought to spread the way to others and his life and teachings are amply recorded by his disciples.

Buddha taught the changing impermanence of the world behind which there was a changeless reality. Events follow from cause and causes give rise to events. Thus all things are related and unchanging reality underlies the world of sense and appearance.

While both the philosophy of the Upanishads and Buddhist philosophy rose from the Law of Karma, the former teachings propound an endless cycle of births and rebirths until the individual soul is freed from the cycle of rebirths by the total end of desire. An individuality persists throughout the long chain of rebirths. According to the Buddhist philosophy, on the other hand, something persists after man's physical body dissolves at death but this something is not individuality. Rather it is the end result of the person's existence and it is this end result or effect which is passed on to and influences other persons.

The scriptural canons of Buddhism are in the Pâli language. A number of years after the death of Buddha, a council was convened to determine which teachings were to be regarded as canonical. Three of the disciples recited the teachings of the Buddha and these recollections were combined to form the "Tripitaka" or "three baskets" (of knowledge) which was finally recorded in writing about 80 B. C.

The Dhammapada, from which the reprint following was taken, constitutes a part of the Buddhistic canon and is said to contain

Buddha's actual utterances.   There are 424 verses in all.   They are arranged in chapters dealing with various subjects, e.g., reflection, thought, evil, punishment, self, the world, happiness, pleasure, anger and so on.

The excerpts following, taken from Max Müller's translation from the Pâli, were accepted as the utterances of the Buddha by the council under Asoka in 246 B. C. — we can hardly expect to get nearer to Buddha himself and his personal teachings.

DHAMMAPADA[1]
(The Path of Virtue)

On Reflection

Reflection is the path of immortality, thoughtlessness the path of death. Those who reflect do not die, those who are thoughtless are as if dead already.

Having understood this clearly, those who are advanced in reflection, delight in reflection, and rejoice in the knowledge of the Arizas (the Elect).

These wise people, meditative, steady, always possessed of strong powers, attain to Nirvâna, the highest happiness.

If a reflecting person has roused himself, if he is not forgetful, if his deeds are pure, if he acts with consideration, if he restrains himself, and lives according to law, — then his glory will increase.

By rousing himself, by reflection, by restraint and control, the wise man may make for himself an island which no flood can overwhelm.

Fools follow after vanity, men of evil wisdom. The wise man possesses reflection as his best jewel.

Follow not after vanity, nor after the enjoyment of love and lust! He who reflects and meditates, obtains ample joy.

When the learned man drives away vanity by reflection, he, the wise, having reached the repose of wisdom, looks down upon the fools, far from toil upon the toiling crowd, as a man who stands on the ground.

Reflecting among the thoughtless, awake among the sleepers, the wise man advances like a racer leaving behind the hack.

By earnestness did Maghavan (Indra) rise to the lordship of the Gods. People praise earnestness; thoughtlessness is always blamed.

A Bhikshu (mendicant) who delights in reflection, who looks with fear on thoughtlessness, moves about like fire, burning all his fetters, small or large.

A Bhikshu (mendicant) who delights in reflection, who looks with fear on thoughtlessness, will not go to destruction — he is near to Nirvâna.

The Wise Man

If you see an intelligent man who tells you where true treasures are to be found, who shows what is to be avoided, and who administers reproofs, follow that wise man; it will be better, not worse, for those who follow him.

Let him admonish, let him command, let him hold back from what is improper! — he will be beloved of the good, by the bad he will be hated.

Do not have evil-doers for friends, do not have low people: have virtuous people for friends, have for friends the best of men.

He who drinks in the Law lives happily with a serene mind: the sage rejoices always in the Law, as preached by the elect.

Well-makers lead the water wherever they like; fletchers bend the arrow; carpenters bend a log of wood; wise people fashion themselves.

As a solid rock is not shaken by the wind, wise people falter not amidst blame and praise.

Wise people, after they have listened to the laws, become serene, like a deep, smooth, and still lake.

Good people walk on whatever befall, the good do not murmur, longing for pleasure; whether touched by happiness or sorrow. Wise people never appear elated or depressed.

If, whether for his own sake, or for the sake of others, a man wishes neither for a son, nor for wealth, nor for lordship, and if he does not wish for his own success by unfair means, then he is good, wise and virtuous . . .

Those whose mind is well grounded in the elements of knowledge, who have given up all attachments, and rejoice without clinging to anything, those whose frailities have been conquered, and who are full of light, are free (even) in this world.

The World

Do not follow the evil law! Do not live on in thoughtlessness! Do not follow false doctrine! Be not a friend of the world.

Rouse thyself! Do not be idle! Follow the law of virtue! The virtuous lives happily in this world and in the next.

Follow the law of virtue; do not follow that of sin. The virtuous lives happily in this world and in the next.

Look upon the world as a bubble, look upon it as a mirage: the king of death does not see him who thus looks down upon the world.

Come, look at this glittering world, like unto a royal chariot; the foolish are immersed in it, but the wise do not cling to it.

He who formerly was reckless and afterwards became sober, brightens up this world, like the moon when freed from clouds.

He whose evil deeds are covered by good deeds, brightens up this world, like the moon when freed from clouds.

This world is dark, few only can see here; a few only go to heaven, like birds escaped from the net.

The swans go on the path of the sun, they go through the ether by means of their miraculous power; the wise are led out of this world, when they have conquered Mâra and his train.

If a man has transgressed one law, and speaks lies, and scoffs at another world, there is no evil he will not do.

The uncharitable do not go to the world of the gods; fools only do not praise liberality; a wise man rejoices in liberality, and through it becomes blessed in the other world.

Better than sovereignty over the earth, better than going to heaven, better than lordship over all worlds, is the reward of the first step in holiness.

---

[1] Max Müller, *Lectures on the Science of Religion; With a Paper on Buddhist Nihilism and a Translation of the Dhammapada or "Path of Virtue."* (New York: Charles Scribner and Company, 1872), pp. 241-242. Reprinted with the permission of the publishers.

BARDO THODOL

Buddhism entered Tibet in the middle of the seventh century. One of the most interesting of the ancient philosophical documents to come out of the Orient is the Tibetan Book of the Dead. It was compiled by the early Buddhists in the first centuries of Lamaism (ca. 50 A. D. and the years following) and provides instruction on the science of death. It was written as a guide book for the dying and contains detailed instructions for their conduct during the forty-nine days before reincarnation and union with the Divine. In accordance with the teachings of the Tibetan Buddhists, the Bardo Thödol is read to the dying as he passes into the Unkonwn Land.

The Bardo Thödol is available in an excellent English translation by Dr. Evans-Wentz who collaborated with the learned Lama Kazi Dawa-Samdup in rendering it into our language. The excerpts following, taken from the translation just mentioned, can provide but the slightest appreciation of this very remarkable book.

BARDO THODOL[1]

O nobly born, the time has now come for you to seek the Path of Reality.   Your breathing is about to cease.

Your teacher has set you face to face with the Clear Light, and now you are about to experience it in its reality, wherein all things are like the void and cloudless sky, and the naked spotless intellect resembles a transparent vacuum without circumference or center.

At this moment know Yourself and abide in that state.

O nobly born, that which is called Death being now come to you, resolve thus:

"O, this is now the hour of death!   By taking advantage of this death I will so act for the good of all sentient beings as to obtain the Perfect Awakening by resolving on love and compassion toward them and by directing my effort to the Sole Perfection."

Reverend sir, now that you are experiencing the Clear Light, try to abide in that state.   Recognize it, O nobly born, listen!

Your present intellect is the Very Reality, the All Good.   Recognize the voidness of your intellect, for that is Awakening, and so keep yourself in the Divine Mind of the Buddha.

Death comes to all.   Do not cling in fondness or weakness to this life.   There is no power in you to remain here.   Be not attached to this world.   Be not weak.   Remember the Holy Trinity of the Buddha, the Law, and the Assembly.   Bearing these words in heart, go forward.

When your body and mind were separating you experiencing a glimpse of the Pure Truth, subtle, sparkling, bright, glorious, and radiantly awful; in appearance like a mirage moving across a landscape in springtime, in one ceaseless flow of vibrations.   Be not daunted nor terrified nor awed.   That is the radiance of your own true nature.   Realize it!

From the midst of that Radiance, roaring like a thousand thunders, Reality will come.   That is the sound of your own True Self.   Be not daunted.

Since you have no longer a material body, sounds, lights, and rays cannot hurt you, harm you.   It is sufficient for you to know that all apparitions are but your own thought-forms.

---

[1] Evans-Wentz, *The Tibetan Book of the Dead* (London: Oxford University Press, 1927).

O nobly born, if you do not now recognize your own thought-forms, the lights will daunt you, the sounds will awe you, the rays will terrify you. Should you not understand this you will have to wander in rebirth.

———o———

CONFUCIUS

Confucius (the Latinized form of K'ung Fu Tsze), styled by a Manchu emperor as the "Perfect Sage," was born in the province of Lu (present Shangtung) in ancient China, in the year 557 B.C. He descended from an old family once noted for its wisdom and valor.

Although little is known of his youth, we know that Confucius dedicated himself, at twenty-two, to the acquisition of wisdom, and started along the path that he was to follow for half a century to become the most illustrious of the Chinese sages.

He traveled from state to state offering his services to the reigning princes. Surrounded by a group of his disciples, he wandered through the provinces of Lu, C'hi, Wei and Ch'in. He taught the principles of the Chou culture, poetry, music, history and the ceremonies. He taught loyalty to self and charity to others. He instilled in his followers the virtues of justice, sincerity, courtesy, benevolence and respect. He sought to combine ability and virtue with high public office, (how like Plato's doctrine of the philosopher-king), and hoped to bring humanity to the elevated plane of existence which an acceptance of the lofty ideals of his ethical system would provide. One commentator has remarked of the teachings of Confucius, that they provide instruction on how to live a life like a gentleman. Despite his aspirations, Confucius held public office for a relatively short period. The accounts of his death record as his last remark his regret that no prince had employed his services for the betterment of the people.

Discouraged by his failure to practically apply his doctrines in governmental office, bereft of his son and virtually unhonored, Confucius passed away in 479 B.C.

Ch'un Ch'in (Spring and Autumn) is the only book generally accredited to his authorship, although there are many others written by his disciples and commentators and filled with his sayings and wisdom. Most important of these are the *Lun Yü* (The Analects), a collection of conversations assembled by Confucius' followers after his death, *The Great Learning, The Doctrine of the Mean, and the sayings* of *Mencius,* the great apostle of Confucianism who lived two centuries after the master.

To attempt to capsulate even a minor segment of Confucius' teachings in the excerpts which follow, is an obvious impossibility. However, the aphorisms which are offered here may provide a general indication of the depth and character of Confucian thought, and certainly they provide abundant ground for thoughtful contemplation.

The excerpts were taken from Dr. James Legge's excellent translation of the *Lun Yü* (The Analects) as published in *The Sacred Books of the East.*

THE ANALECTS[1]

A youth, when at home, should be filial, and, abroad, respectful to his elders. He should be earnest and truthful. He should overflow in love to all, and cultivate the friendship of the good.

If a man keeps cherishing his old knowledge, so as continually to be acquiring new, he may be a teacher of others.

Learning without thought is labour lost; thought without learning is perilous.

When you know a thing, to hold that you know it; and when you do not know a thing, to allow that you do not know it—this is knowledge.

To see what is right and not to do it is want of courage.

Those who are without virtue cannot abide long either in condition of poverty and hardship, or in a condition of enjoyment. The virtuous rest in virtue; the wise desire virtue.

The superior man, in the world, does not set his mind either for anything, or against anything; what is right he will follow.

The superior man thinks of virtue; the small man thinks of comfort.

When we see men of worth, we should think of equalling them; when we see men of a contrary character, we should turn inwards and examine ourselves.

What I do not wish men to do to me, I also wish not to do to men.

Hearing much and selecting what is good and following it; seeing much and keeping it in memory—this is the second style of knowledge.

When a country is well-governed, poverty and a mean condition are things to be ashamed of. When a country is ill-governed, riches and honours are things to be ashamed of.

Learn as if you could not reach your object, and were always fearing also lest you should lose it.

I have not seen one who loves virtue as he loves beauty.

Hold faithfulness and sincerity as first principles. Have no friends not equal to yourself. When you have faults, do not fear to abandon them.

The wise are free from perpexities; the virtuous from anxiety; and the bold from fear.

To subdue one's self and return to propriety, is perfect virtue.

The man of perfect virtue is cautious and slow in his speech.

The requisites of government are that there be sufficiency of food, sufficiency of military equipment, and the confidence of the people in their ruler.

The superior man seeks to perfect the admirable qualities of men, and does not seek to perfect their bad qualities.

Good government obtains, when those who are near are made happy, and those who are far off are attracted.

Do not be desirous to have things done quickly; do not look at small advantages. Desire to have things done quickly prevents their being done thoroughly. Looking at small advantages prevents great affairs from being accomplished.

The superior man is affable, but not adulatory; the mean man is adulatory, but not affable.

The superior man has a dignified ease without pride. The mean man has pride without a dignified ease.

Superior men, and yet not always virtuous, there have been, alas! But there never has been a mean man, and, at the same time virtuous.

He who speaks without modesty will find it difficult to make his words good.

Recompense injury with justice, and recompense kindness with kindness.

If a man take no thought about what is distant, he will find sorrow near at hand.

He who requires much from himself and little from others, will keep himself from being the object of resentment.

What the superior man seeks, is in himself. What the mean man seeks, is in others.

The superior man is correctly firm, and not firm merely.

There are three friendships which are advantageous, and three which are injurious. Friendship with the upright; friendship with the sincere; and friendship with the man of much observation—these are advantageous. Friendship with the man of specious airs; friendship with the insinuatingly soft; and friendship with the glib-tongued—these are injurious.

By nature, men are nearly alike; by practice, they get to be wide apart.

There are only the wise of the highest class, and the stupid of the lowest class, who cannot be changed.

---

1 Reprinted from James Legge, *The Chinese Classics*, Vol. I, (Oxford: Clarendon Press, 1893), pp. 137 ff.

LAO TZU

Lao Tzu (pronounced "loudza"), the Chinese mystic and founder of Taoism, was a contemporary of Confucius, and many accounts indicate that the two actually met on one occasion.

Little is known of his life, and much that is to be found in the historical records is so bound up with legend as to cast a shadow over its accuracy. We may be certain, however, that he was a man of great learning and wisdom. It is believed that Lao Tzu was a native of Chu, in the south of China (now the province of Honan), and there he sought to preserve the culture of the suppressed people of Yin just as Confucius was attempting to preserve the culture of the ruling people of Chou. Whether or not he traveled to India, which might be indicated by the nature and tone of his teachings, is debatable in the absence of more exact records of the facts of his life.

The teachings of Lao Tzu are more spiritual, though less popular, than those of Confucius. In his short book, the *Tao Teh King*, there is to be found a wisdom reminiscent of the dazzling spiritual truths that have come from ancient India. In this work, which is variously translated as *The Way and Virtue* or *The Canon of Reason and Virtue*, there is a transcendental philosophy partaking of many elements which are also found in the teachings of the Indian philosophers. Thus, there is the belief in reincarnation, in the doctrine of a monistic universe, and in the idea that the divine transcends good and evil. Lao Tzu even expresses the substance of Indian Yoga when he refers to concentration as "a way to knowledge."

Taoism (*Tao* means "the way," or "the principle," or "nature") was founded by Lao Tzu and propounded by Chuang Tzu and many others. It teaches that this Tao is of an elusive, vague character not dissimilar to that credited to the universe in Indian speculative thought. Of it Lao Tzu says, "there is in it the form and the essence," of nature. The Taoists taught that men should act in harmony with this unseen Tao. Their teachings inculcate a belief in the underlying unity of all things, and suggest that by a careful study of principles observable in nature, the fundamental or refined essence of reality may be seen, as contrasted to the coarse embodiment of reality in things as such.

The Taoist religion (*Tao chiao*) arose during the Han dynasty (206 B.C.—220 A.D.) from these teachings of Lao Tzu.

The excerpts reprinted here were taken form the first ten chapters of the *Tao Teh King* as it appears, in translation, in the *Sacred Books of China*.

TAO TEH KING[1]

The Tao that can be trodden is not the enduring and unchanging Tao. The name that can be named is not the enduring and unchanging name.

Conceived of as having no name, it is the originator of heaven and earth; conceived of as having a name, it is the mother of all things.

> Always without desire we must be found,
> If its deep mystery we would sound;
> But if desire always within us be,
> Its outer fringe is all that we shall see.

Under these two aspects, it is really the same; but as development takes place, it receives the different names. Together we call them the Mystery. Where the Mystery is the deepest is the gate of all that is subtle and wonderful.

All in the world know the beauty of the beautiful, and in doing this they have the idea of what ugliness is; they all know the skill of the skillful, and in doing this they have the idea of what the want of skill is.

So it is that existence and non-existence give birth the one to the idea of the other; that difficulty and ease produce the one the idea of the other; that length and shortness fashion out the one the figure of the other; that the ideas of height and lowness arise from the contrast of the one with the other; that the musical notes and tones become harmonious through the relation of one with the other; and that being before and behind give the idea of one following another.

Therefore the sage manages affairs without doing anything, and conveys his instructions without the use of speech.

All things spring up, and there is not one which declines to show itself; they grow, and there is no claim for their ownership; they go through their processes, and there is no expectation of a reward for the results. The work is accomplished, and there is no resting in it as an achievement.

> The work is done, but how no one can see;
> 'Tis this that makes the power not cease to be.

Not to value and employ men of superior ability is the way to keep the people from rivalry among themselves; not to prize articles which are difficult to procure is the way to keep them from becoming thieves; not to show them what is likely to excite their desires is the way to keep their minds from disorder.

Therefore, the sage, in the exercise of his government, empties their minds, fills their bellies, weakens their wills and strengthens their bones.

He constantly tries to keep them without knowledge and without desire, and where there are those who have knowledge, to keep them from presuming to act on it. When this abstinence from action, good order is universal.

The Tao is like the emptiness of a vessel; and in our employment of it we must be on our guard against all fulness. How deep and unfathomable it is, as if it were the Honoured Ancestor of all things!

We should blunt our sharp points, and unravel the complications of things; we should attemper our brightness, and bring ourselves into agreement with the obscurity of others. How pure and still the Tao is, as if it would ever so continue!

I do not know whose son it is. It might appear to have been before God.

Heaven and earth do not act from the impulse of any wish to be benevolent; they deal with all things as the dogs of grass are dealt with. The sages do not act from any wish to be benevolent; they deal with the people as the dogs of grass are dealt with.

May not the space between heaven and earth be compared to a bellows?

'Tis emptied, yet it loses not its power;
'Tis moved again, and sends forth air the more.
Much speech to swift exhaustion lead we see;
Your inner being guard, and keep it free.
The valley spirit dies not, aye the same;
The female mystery thus do we name.
Its gate, from which at first they issued forth,
Is called the root from which grew heaven and earth.
Long and unbroken does its power remain,
Used gently, and without the touch of pain.

Heaven is long-enduring and earth continues long. The reason why heaven and earth are able to endure and continue thus long is because they do not live of, or for, themselves. This is how they are able to continue and endure.

Therefore the sage puts his own person last, and yet it is found in the foremost place; he treats his person as if it were foreign to him, and yet that person is preserved. Is it not because he has no personal and private ends, that therefore such ends are realized?

The highest excellence is like that of water. The excellence of water appears in its benefiting all things, and in its occupying, without striving to the contrary, the low place which all men dislike. Hence its way is near to that of the Tao.

The excellence of a residence is in the suitability of the place; that of the mind is in abysmal stillness; that of associations is in their being with the virtuous; that of government is in its securing good order; that of the conduct of affairs is in its ability; and that of the initiation of any movement is in its timeliness.

And when one with the highest excellence does not wrangle about his low position, no one finds fault with him.

It is better to leave a vessel unfilled, than to attempt to carry it when it is full. If you keep feeling a point that has been sharpened, the point cannot long preserve its sharpness.

When gold and jade fill the hall, their possessor cannot keep them safe. When wealth and honours lead to arrogancy, this brings its evil on itself. When the work is done and one's name is becoming distinguished, to withdraw into obscurity is the way of Heaven.

When the intelligent and animal souls are held together in one embrace, they can be kept from separating. When one gives undivided attention to the vital breath, and brings it to the utmost degree of pliancy, he can become as a tender babe. When he has cleansed away the most mysterious sights of his imagination, he can become without a flaw.

In loving the people and ruling the state, cannot he proceed without any purpose of action? In the opening and shutting of his gates of heaven, cannot he do so as a female bird? While his intelligence reaches in every direction, cannot he appear to be without knowledge.

The Tao produces all things and nourishes them; it produces them and does not claim them as its own; it does all, and yet does not boast of it; it presides over all, and yet does not control them. This is what is called 'The Mysterious Quality' of the Tao.

----

1 Reprinted from James Legge, *The Sacred Books of China: The Texts of Taoism,* Part 1. (Oxford: Clarendon Press, 1891), pp 47 ff.

CHUANG TZU

Lao Tsu's greatest disciple was Chuang Tzu (pronounced "chwong-dza"), born in the fourth century B.C. in the Chinese province of An-hui.

His writings reflect a cool cynicism, and his keen imagination together with his exquisite style have provided as interesting reading as any to be found in Oriental Philosophy. Chuang Tzu was no mere reciter of the doctrines of his master, for he added much and developed his own thought, although his fundamental teachings reflect those of his preceptor.

Chuang Tzu taught the oneness of the universe, the singularity of opposites (by which is meant that the good, for example, is significant only in relation to the bad), and the belief that only from the subjective do we gain insight into the nature of objective reality. Seeking to merge the spiritual and the material, the two masters of Taoism left much of beauty and value in their writings. Present day Taoism scarcely indicates the nobility and spiritual profundity of the doctrines of its ancient founders.

The ablest scholar of his day, those of whom he wrote could neither escape nor reply to his satire. In refusing high office in the court of King Wei of Khu, Chuang Tau compared the position he would hold if he were to take the proffered office, to that of the oxen which is fed well before it enters the temple to be sacrificed on the altar.

The excerpts following consist of parts of Books III and XV of the writings of Chuang Tzu as they appear in Legge's translation of the texts of Taoism. Book III, "Nourishing the Lord of Life," sets forth the idea that the Tao may be best nourished by the avoidance of all striving to do so; by a passionless performance of the duties of our position in life; and by accepting the Tao as a guide in our actions with a full resignation to the inevitable decay and death of our being. Book XV, translated by Legge as "Ingrained Ideas," sets forth the notions so commonly held by men as to be thought almost inherent in the human mind. It describes six classes of men, only one of which includes the true followers of Taoism. It characterizes the sage and true Taoist as a man possessing a pure simplicity in pursuing "the Way."

THE WRITINGS OF CHUANG TZU[1]

Yang Shang Ku, or Nourishing the Lord of Life

There is a limit to our life, but to knowledge there is no limit. With what is limited to pursue after what is unlimited is a perilous thing; and when, knowing this, we still seek the increase of our knowledge, the peril cannot be averted. There should not be the practice of what is good with any thought of fame which it will bring, nor of what is evil with any approximation to the punishment which it will incur—an accordance with the central element of our nature is the regular way to preserve the body, to maintain the life, to nourish our parents, and to complete our term of years.

His cook was cutting up an ox for the ruler Wan-hui. Whenever he applied his hand, leaned forward with his shoulder, planted his foot, and employed the pressure of his knee, in the audible ripping off of the skin, and slicing operation of the knife, the sounds were all in regular cadence. Movements and sounds proceeded as in the dance of 'The Mulberry Forest' and the blended notes of 'The King Shau.' The ruler said, 'Ah! Admirable! That your art should have become so perfect!' Having finished his operation, the cook laid down his knife, and replied to the remark, 'What your servant loves is the method of the Tao, something in advance of any art. When I first began to cut up an ox, I saw nothing but the entire carcase. After three years I ceased to see it as a whole. Now I deal with it in a spirit-like manner, and do not look at it with my eyes. The use of my senses is discarded, and my spirit acts as it wills. Observing the natural lines, my knife slips through the great crevices and slides through the great cavities, taking advantage of the facilities thus presented. My art avoids the membraneous ligatures, and much more the great bones.

'A good cook changes his knife every year;—it may have been injured in cutting; an ordinary cook changes his every month;—it may have been broken. Now my knife has been in use for nineteen years; it has cut up several thousand oxen, and yet its edge is as sharp as if it had newly come from the whetstone. There are the interstices of the joints, and the edge of the knife has no appreciable thickness; when that which is so thin enters where the interstice is, how easily it moves along! The blade has more than room enough. Nevertheless, whenever I come to a complicated joint, and see that there will be some difficulty, I proceed anxiously and with caution, not allowing my eyes to wander from the place, and moving my hand slowly. Then by a very slight movement of the knife, the part is quickly separated, and drops like a clod of earth to the ground. Then standing up with the knife in my hand, I look all around, and in a leisurely manner, with an air of satisfaction, wipe it clean, and put it in its sheath.' The ruler Wan-hui said, 'Excellent! I have heard the words of my cook, and learned from them the nourishment of our life.'

Kho I, or Ingrained Ideas

Ingrained ideas and a high estimate of their own conduct; leaving the world, and pursuing uncommon ways; talking loftily and in resentful disparagement of others;—all this is simply symptomatic of arrogance. This is what scholars who betake themselves to the hills and valleys, who are always blaming the world, and who stand aloof like withered trees, or throw themselves into deep pools, are fond of.

Discoursing of benevolence, righteousness, loyalty, and good faith; being humble and frugal, self-forgetful and courteous;—all this is simply symptomatic of self-cultivation. This is what scholars who wish to tranquillise the world, teachers and instructors, men who pursue their studies at home and abroad, are fond of.

Discoursing of their great merit and making a great name for themselves; insisting on the ceremonies between ruler and minister; and rectifying the relations between high and low;—all this shows their one object to be the promotion of government. This is what officers of the court, men who honour their lord and would strengthen the state and who would do their utmost to incorporate other states with their own, are fond of.

Resorting to marshes and lakes; dwelling in solitary places; occupying themselves with angling and living at ease;—all this shows their one object to be to do nothing. This is what gentlemen of the rivers and seas, men who avoid the society of the world and desire to live at leisure, are fond of.

Blowing and breathing with open mouth; inhaling and exhaling the breath; expelling the old breath and taking in new; passing their time like the dormant bear, and stretching and twisting the neck like a bird;—all this simply shows the desire for longevity. This is what the scholars who manipulate the breath, and the men who nourish the body and wish to live as long as Pang Zû, are fond of.

As to those who have a lofty character without any ingrained ideas; who pursue the path of self cultivation without benevolence and righteousness; who succeed in government without great services or fame; who enjoy their ease without resorting to the rivers or seas; who attain to longevity without the management of the breath; who forget all things and yet possess all things; whose placidity is unlimited, while all things to be valued attend them: — such men pursue the way of heaven and earth, and display the characteristics of the sages. Hence it is said, 'Placidity, indifference, silence, quietude, absolute vacancy, and non-action: — these are the qualities which maintain the level of heaven and earth and are the substance of the Tao and its characteristics.'

In accordance with this it is said, 'The sage is entirely restful, and so his mind is evenly balanced and at ease. This even balance and ease appears in his placidity and indifference. In this state of even balance and ease, of placidity and indifference, anxieties and evils do not find access to him, no depraving influence can take him by surprise; his virtue is complete, and his spirit continues unimpaired.'

Therefore it is said further, 'Sadness and pleasure show a depraving element in the virtue of those who feel them; joy and anger show some error in their course; love and hatred show a failure of virtue. Hence for the mind to be free from sorrow and pleasure is the perfection of virtue; to be of one mind that does not change is the perfection of quietude; to be conscious of no opposition is the perfection of indifference; and to have no rebellious dissatisfactions is the perfection of purity.'

There is the vulgar saying, 'The multitude of men consider gain to be the most important thing; pure scholars, fame; those who are wise and able value their ambition; the sage prizes essential purity.' Therefore simplicity is the denomination of that in which there is no admixture; purity of that in which the spirit is not impaired. It is he who can embody simplicity and purity whom we call the True Man.

---

[1] Reprinted from James Legge, *The Sacred Books of China: The Texts of Taoism*, Part I (Oxford: Clarendon Press, 1891), pp. 198-202 and 363-367.

MENCIUS

Mencius, or Meng Tsu, was born in the province of Lu, in China, in the year 371 B.C. He closed the period in which the great intellectual achievements of the Buddha, Confucius and Lao Tsu were made. After him, the torch of philosophy, dimming in the Orient, assumed a new brilliance on the far-away Attic peninsula with the early Grecian philosophers.

Mencius studied under Tsu Ssu, grandson of Confucius, and held office for a time as advisor to the governing prince of Ch'i. Later, he traveled from one province to another, and at length betook himself to the company of his disciples, to teach and study.

His teachings represent the so-called "orthodox" school of Confucian thought. In the *Book of Mencius,* the thought of Confucius is developed clearly and even eloquently. Numerous of the aphoristic statements in *The Analects* are to be found expanded into lengthy expositions of the philosophic values represented.

Mencius gave first importance to the idea of the goodness of human nature, and the basic equality of men in the original possession of this goodness. The positive qualities of a man, he believed exist originally in that man, and their absence is the result of a neglect to cultivate and restore them. If the individual loses his moral consciousness of good and evil, he sinks to the level of the beast.

Mencius also sets forth the Confucian ideal of government, and distinguishes between what we might term the "virtuous ruler" as opposed to the ruler who seizes his power by force.

The following excerpts of the wisdom of this great Confucian were taken from *The Life and Works of Mencius,* Vol. II, as translated by James Legge. Chapter VII, following, is concerned with the phenomena of good and evil in men's character and conduct as explained by the varied influences acting on them. Chapter VIII explains how it is that nature properly good comes to appear otherwise from not receiving proper nourishment. Chapter IX, in Mencius, illustrates the points made in Chapter VIII and has been omitted here as has been the next chapter, which discourses on man's nature to love righteousness. Chapter XI shows how man, having lost the proper qualities of his nature, should seek to recover them, and the last excerpt, Chapter XII, considers how men are sensible to bodily defects but insensible to mental and moral ones.

THE BOOK OF MENCIUS[1]

Ch. VII. Mencius said, "In good years the children of the people are most of them good, and in bad years they are most of them evil. It is not owing to their natural endowments conferred by Heaven, that they are thus different. It is owing to the circumstances in which they allow their minds to be ensnared and devoured that they appear so as in the latter case.

"Now there is barley.—Let the seed be sown and covered up; the ground being the same, and the time being also the same, it grows luxuriantly, and when the full time is come, it is all found to be ripe. Although there may be inequalities of produce, that is owing to the difference of the soil as rich or poor, to the unequal nourishment afforded by rain and dew, and to the different ways in which man has performed his business.

"Thus all things which are the same in kind are like to one another; —why should we doubt in regard to man, as if he were a solitary expection to this? The sage and we are the same in kind.

"In accordance with this, Lung-tsze said, 'If a man make hempen sandals, without knowing the size of people's feet, yet I know that he will not make them like baskets.' Sandals are like one another, because all men's feet are like one another.

"So with the mouth and flavours;—all mouths have the same relishes. Yih Ya (*a famous cook.* Ed.) simply appreciated before me what my mouth relishes. Suppose that his mouth, in its relish for flavours, were of a different nature from the mouths of other men, in the same way as dogs and horses are not of the same kind with us, how should all men be found following Yih Ya in their relishes? In the matter of tastes, the whole kingdom models itself after Yih Ya; that is, the mouths of all men are alike one another.

"So it is with the ear also. In the matter of sounds, the whole kingdom models itself after the music-master Kwang; that is, the ears of all men are like one another.

"And so it is also with the eye. In the case of Tsze, there is no one under heaven but who would recognize that he was beautiful. Anyone who did not recognize the beauty of Tsze—too would be said to have no eyes.

"Therefore I say,—Men's mouths agree in having the same relishes; their ears agree in enjoying the same sounds; their eyes agree in recognizing the same beauty: — shall their minds alone be without that which they similarly approve? What is it then of which their minds similarly approve? It is the principles of things, and the consequent

determinations of righteousness. The sages only apprehended before
me that which I and other men agree in approving. Therefore the
principles of things and the determination of righteousness are agreeable to my mind just as the flesh of grass and grain fed animals is
agreeable to my mouth.

Ch. VIII. Mencius said, "The trees of New Hill were once beautiful. Being situated, however, in the suburbs of the capital of a large
State, they were hewn down with axes and bills; and could they retain
their beauty? Still through the growth from the vegetative life day and
night, and the nourishing influence of the rain and dew, they were not
without buds and sprouts springing out. But then came the cattle and
goats, and browsed upon them. To these things is owing the bare and
stript appearance of the hill; and when people see this, they think it
was never finely wooded. But is this the nature of the hill?

"And so even of what properly belongs to man; shall it be said
that the mind of any man was without benevolence and righteousness.
The way in which a man loses the proper goodness and righteousness. The way in which a man loses the proper goodness of his mind
is like the way in which those trees were denuded by axes and bills.
Hewn down day after day, can it retain its excellence? But there is
some growth of its life day and night, and in the calm air of the
morning, just between night and day, the mind feels in a degree those
desires and aversions which are proper to humanity; but the feeling
is not strong; and then it is fettered and destroyed by what the man
does during the day. This fettering takes place again and again; the
restorative influence of the night is not sufficient to preserve the proper
goodness; and when this proves insufficient for that purpose, the
nature becomes not much different from that of irrational animals;
and when people see this, they think that it never had those endowments which I assert. But does this condition represent the feelings
proper to humanity?

"Therefore if it receive its proper nourishment, there is nothing
which will not grow; if it lose its proper nourishment, there is nothing
which will not decay away.

"Confucius said, 'Hold it fast, and it remains with you; let it go,
and you lose it. Its out-going and in-coming cannot be defined as to
time and place.' It was the mental nature of which this was said."

Ch. XI. Mencius said, "Benevolence is the proper quality of man's
mind, and righteousness is man's proper path.

"How lamentable is it to neglect this path and not pursue it, to lose
this mind and not know to seek it again.

"When men's fowls and dogs are lost, they know to seek them

again; but they lose their mind, and do not know to seek it again.

"The object of learning is nothing else but to seek for the lost mind."

Ch. XII. Mencius said, "Here is a man whose fourth finger is bent, and cannot be stretched out straight. It is not painful, nor does it incommode his business; but if there were anyone who could make it straight, he would not think it far to go all the way from T'sin to Ts'oo to find him;—because his finger is not like those of other people.

"When a man's finger is not like other people's, he knows to feel dissatisfied; but when his mind is not like other people's, he does not know to feel dissatisfied. This is what is called ignorance of the relative importance of things.

---

[1] Reprinted from James Legge, *The Chinese Classics: The Life and Works of Mencius*, Vol. II. (London: Trubner & Co., 1875)

Printed in the United States
141959LV00006B/80/A

9 781417 977550